In loving memory
of my parents,
Edith Ardena Coleman Thomas

&

for Randy "Guru" Atkins,
Mike "Dr. Cone" Cone
Doug "Bro" Herrera
and Bob "Johnnybob, Jr." Spears
lanterns in the darkness

TABLE OF CONTENTS

I. HARD PRAYER

II. THEIR EYES ALL PUPIL

Where Skulls Speak Wind

Larry D. Thomas

Texas Review Press
Huntsville, Texas

FIRST EDITION, 2004

Requests for permission to reproduce material from this work should be sent to:

Permissions
Texas Review Press
English Department
Sam Houston State University
Huntsville, TX 77341-2146

ACKNOWLEDGMENTS

The author offers grateful acknowledgment to the editors of the following publications in which the poems herein were originally published, sometimes in slightly different versions:

Amarillo Bay, American Indian Culture and Research Journal, Black Bear Review, Blue Violin, Borderlands: Texas Poetry Review, Brazos River Review, Cape Rock, Chattahoochee Review, Chili Verde Review, Christian Science Monitor, Concho River Review, Curbside Review, descant: Fort Worth's Journal of Poetry and Fiction, Desert Candle, Earth's Daughters, Equine Image, Journal of the American Medical Association, Midwest Quarterly, New Texas 2001, New Texas 2002, Plainsongs, Poetry Depth Quarterly, RE:AL, Red River Review, Rio Grande Review, RiverSedge, San Antonio Current, Small Pond Magazine of Literature, Southwestern American Literature, Sulphur River Literary Review, Texas Longhorn Trails, Western and Cowboy Poetry at the BAR-D Ranch, Whole Notes, Windhover and *Writers' Forum.*

"Alzheimer's." *JAMA: The Journal of the American Medical Association* 284: No. 3 (2000): 280. Copyright 2000, American Medical Association.

"Checkers." *The Small Pond Magazine of Literature* Vol. XL, No. 1 (117), Beinecke Rare Book & Manuscript Library, Yale University. Copyright 2003, Napoleon St. Cyr, Editor/Publisher.

"Of This Moment." *The Christian Science Monitor* June 21, 2002. Copyright 2002, The Christian Science Publishing Society.

"Out of the Blue." *San Antonio Current* November 15-21, 2001. Copyright 2001, San Antonio Current Company.

"Bluing" was selected by *Plainsongs* poetry journal as a *Plainsongs Award Poem.* "A Place in the Sun" was nominated for the Pushcart Prize by *RE:AL, The Journal of Liberal Arts.*

Cover photograph by Lisa Thomas

Library of Congress Cataloging-in-Publication Data
Thomas, Larry D., 1947—
    Where skulls speak wind / Larry D. Thomas. — 1st ed.
    p. cm.
    ISBN 1-881515-64-8 (alk. paper)
    1. Texas, West—Poetry. I. Title
    PS3620.H63W48 2004
    811'.6—dc22

                                            2004004282

III. OUT OF THE BLUE

IV. WITH THE HAND OF THE GREAT SPIRIT

V. FROM THE ROLL UP YONDER

I. HARD PRAYER

Wind

circa 1880, West Texas

It died down to a zephyr
but would never, never stop.
All they did was listen
and grace it now and then
with psalms and gospels.
Its dogged struggle

was a perfect metaphor
for their faith, the manner,
even for their memory,
in which it kept after them,
sanding their gravestones
night and day to dust.

When the sky greened and it rose,
in case it made a cyclone,
they grabbed their kids and hurried
down the steps of their cellars,
armed with but hard prayer
to foil the howling darkness.

The River

Even before they were born,
their plots were laid out
in the only cemetery.
The men worked the land
of their fathers.
The women, obedient as sheep,
bore them many children.
The sons shaped their feet
with the shoes of their fathers.
To the plight of their mothers,
the daughters surrendered their dreams.

For the people and their livestock,
the river was the source
of life-giving water.
Nights, late in their lives,
when they heard the river
sluicing through the hearts of the farms,
the wives loosed themselves
from the chains of their frozen bodies,
drifted to the river's edge,
and launched their secret, ghostly boats
creaking with the cargo of desire.

Crosses

In the graveyard
at Terlingua,
by the dozens, they lie
stacked atop their graves

as if for burning.
The ever present wind,
persistent as a dentist
prying an incisor

from its socket with forceps,
first dismantled
their transverses
then worked their uprights

back and forth for decades
till they fell.
The last caretaker,
a lifelong native,

just left them there,
knowing, even if
he'd tried to stop it,
the wind would always win.

The Cyclone

It tore through the farms
like the vortex of hell itself.
The jars of jellies
and blanched vegetables
clattered on the shelves
carved into the dark earthen walls
of the storm cellars.

To camouflage their trembling,
the husbands clung to their wives.
The wives, calm as stone,
comforted the children,
the storm raging above
pale beside the silent ones
trapped inside their hearts.

Grandmother Worrell

for Jack

Near the end of a heat wave
at the turn of the century,
some kids took sick in West Texas.

They lived in a shack
roofed with corrugated metal
hot enough with sun

to fry a raw egg.
With black axle grease
she smeared their little chests

in an ages old remedy
she learned from a dead relative.
The shack was an oven

where the sick kids lay
baking with high fever
like homemade biscuits.

Under her sunbonnet
she kept her vigil
rocking beside the blackened brood,

her snuff-stained, stiff upper lip
and hard, hard prayer
all that was left to save them.

O'Keeffe's Skulls

She gathered them
from her Ghost Ranch landscape
and kept them
for her canvases,
haunting remnants
of elk, horse, steer, deer
and ram.

Though decades past, Death
had had its way with them
and the sun had bleached them
beyond whiteness, they still
held in their lasting
a terrible grace.

For this she loved them
and the selfless way
they rendered
when juxtaposed in art
beside her flowers,
each so awfully fresh.

In Far West Texas

the night sky
hogs all the elegance,
a black velvet
jeweler's cloth
roiling with diamonds.

The land has no room
for pretense,
a vast expanse
of rock, dust and thorn
naked to the sun.

The bleached skulls
of cattle
are its oracles,
speaking nothing
but the wind

of this sun-
baked place
where the cowboy's
anything but urban
or drugstore.

Guadalupe Pass

Wind, in January,
at Guadalupe Pass
in far West Texas,
reaches speeds

exceeding
one hundred ten
miles per hour;
howls

like a pack
of wolves;
rips,
as if with pliers,

thorns from the flesh
of cacti;
turns noon sky
the color of dried blood;

and pits the paint
of new pickups,
pregnant as it is
with New Mexico.

Poor Souls

Some say the cowboy
is passé, gone the way
of buggy, quill and candle;

that the only chaps now
are buckled to the dust-
collecting legs

of mannequins in museums,
draping the dreamlike
bones of legend.

Poor souls, these highfalutin
ignoramuses, who,
speeding down the interstate

through far West Texas,
miss Marfa, Alpine,
Fort Davis and Marathon

and their out-of-the-way
cafés abuzz each daybreak
with the drawled price of cattle

and the dull luminosity
of tarnished silver
spur-jangle.

Bull Riders

Like the best ballplayers,
they study percentages,
whether the bulls
buck right or left,
ogling them hawklike
sometimes for years
before they draw
they hope the meanest and wrap
their gloved hand tight with rope.

Though they try to block him out
for better concentration,
Lane's ever in the back
of their mind, Lane Frost,
whom many consider
the best who ever rode
till his last bull
gored his sternum
and snuffed out his life.

They say their sport's addictive,
like the devil
to the bluesman,
that they're all but dead
in the bleak, seemingly
endless intervals
between those electric
eight-second Texas Two-Steps
with the Reaper.

Antique Shop, After Closing

This place, after closing,
is hushed as the tomb
of a Pharaoh,

this place of objects
complete in themselves,
shrine-like,

beyond the selfish reach
of usefulness,
like poems

deconstructed
into the bleached,
solid blocks

of an alphabet
randomly strewn
on a shelf in a place

where nothing moves
but light, shadow,
and dust drifting

downward through the darkness
like the laying on
of hands.

The Worshipers

for Daniel

Clad completely in black,
they sit on their pews
so straight-backed
their profiles loom
like halves of thick swastikas.

Born and reared in West Texas,
they live out the scripts
of black-and-white lives
flawlessly bereft of gray.
Their houseplants are cacti,

armed with thorns to thwart
even the thought
of a vulgar human touch.
Their raw, bony hands
lie folded on their Bibles

placed strategically
atop their iron-
clad thighs, flat
and impenetrable
as distant mesas.

Valentine, Texas

They adorn
their walls
with skulls

picked clean
decades back
by the sleek,

gratuitous
beaks
of buzzards.

Nights,
when the parched
earth's dusted

with the chalklike
film
of moonglow,

even
the music
seeping

from beat-up
pickup trucks
is bleak,

strewn
with the rubble
of broken hearts.

Ghost Town

It's so quiet here
a rustle of wind
is a scream.

What buildings still stand,
like strange, angular hills,
have assumed
the timeless hues
of the landscape.

A saloon door, dark yet
with the greasy
residue of men,
clings to a single hinge.

The clapboards
have cracked and curled,
tugging at nails of rust.

For decades,
like the slow,
deliberate fingers
of archaeologists,
only the shadows
have been moving.

Out Here in Far

West Texas, between Balmorhea
and Van Horn, the hallowed flesh
of Mother Earth is nothing but badlands

peppered with daggers of yucca,
erupting skyward every few miles
to jagged ridges of treeless mountains

shedding their robes of shadow
to broil in late June sun.
With faces of cracked leather,

the cowhands mount hot horses
and ride into the wind-
swept fires of their venerable hell,

their skulls vacuous with sky,
their rawboned human thoughts
sizzling on skewers of dazzling sunlight.

Mercado

The aromas of roses
and the blood of fresh meat
vie for preeminence
in the thick, heavy air.

Pyramids of onions,
busy with their yellows,
water the eyes
of passersby.

Chilies,
overflowing their baskets,
shine, swarming their reds
like beds of angry ants.

The snouts
of severed hogs' heads
whisper the gossip
of death.

Rows of clay pots,
warmed by the sun,
radiate the scent
of the potter.

In a sky of piñatas
dangling from their nooses,
the chickens, iridescent with flies,
swing like the watches of hypnotists.

The Skeleton

Of Mexican clay,
in the classic
Mexican mockery
of death, it hangs
flat against a wall.

Its bones are linked
by copper wire
twisted into ovals.

Its skull slightly
turned toward a window,
it gapes
in the bizarre guffaw
of lockjaw.

Its oversized fingers
dangle well
beneath its knees,
its apelike arms
ludicrous as the reach
of the law.

Poinsettias

in the hour
of night
are growing
in Mexico.
They are growing

in clay pots
cradled in the hands
of widows
kneeling at stations
of the cross.

They are growing
in flower beds
flush against the mud
of humble houses
where children play

in the light
painters love,
the light
of Mexico
where bracts grow skyward

to gods
of sun and moon,
staining the windows
of cathedrals,
lavishing the earth

with blooms
of petaled blood.

Their Little Village

They handle their deaths with flowers
which, even in their dying,
ooze fragrant plenitude,
banner their pleas of love,
and disguise, if only
momentarily, the cold,

metallic glare of the coffin.
They know their little village
will somehow manage to endure,
yawning at each sunrise,
peppering the ancient mountainside
like fragments of a torn piñata,

and that somewhere, in a makeshift
studio, a new artist will bud
to carry on the color,
dragging pastels miraculously
across the coarse, white corpses
of the trees.

II. THEIR EYES ALL PUPIL

Of This Moment

primaveral,
when the trees
are tuning forks

struck into the tones
of birdsong,
the squirrels

descend the trunks
like beads
of hot wax,

each onto the floor
of his own
little room

sans walls or roof,
lit by a thousand
candles

in the dazzling
yellow house
of morning.

The Live Oaks

just loom
moonstruck
at the very edge
of her dreamscape
and wear twilight
like dark green

evening gowns.
She starts to feel
the strength of arms
lifted skyward,
gnarled with the grace
of the ages.

They just loom.
They just wait
for the weightless lives
of roosting sparrows
and their hushed,
jackhammer hearts.

Sparrows

Though their plumage
is anything
but dazzling,
adorned as it is
with nothing
but earth tones

of brown and gray:
though they are common
and seldom if ever
delight the trained eye
of the watcher:
and though

they will never
grace the perch
of a gilded cage,
they still dart
to their feeder.
They puff up

their breasts.
They splay
their tail feathers.
And they fight
with the violence
of lions.

Raven in Snow

Her every move's
a pose
for a masterpiece
of black-and-white
photography.
Having gulped her niece
and half her nephew,

she strops her beak
and rests her belly
in a nest of ice
she can't even feel.
Soon she'll tear her breast
from her pure,
white noun of snow,

take to the wind
and crack the heavens
with her caw,
conjugating
in the brightness
the bold black verb
of her self.

Vultures

To make them
God took
the thick
black fabric
of shadows
and tore it
into shreds.

With the cloths
of their beaks,
they buff
the bones
of the dead
to a fine
white shine,

and they roost,
sagging
the branches
of dead trees
with the droopy,
sated yearnings
of their bodies.

Pinto

A windless place
of blinding
winter sun

on a steep
hillside
near Fort Davis.

A quiet place
where she stands
perfectly still

in fresh,
deep snow
and brown

has never
been as
dazzling.

The Black Stallion

It's midnight,
the sky's moonless,
and in the wind's
the first hint
of fall.

He thunders
to the mesa's brink,
abruptly stops,
flares black nostrils
and sucks

deep into his lungs
the electric
blue-blackness
of the night.
He rears

and paws the heavens
with his forelegs.
His black hooves
glint for a moment
with starlight

and crash
to the earth
like smoldering
black meteorites,
quaking Texas.

Longhorns in Summer

The land where they stand
is glowing iron bracing itself
for the raised hammer of a blacksmith.

They've stood in Texas sun
since the 1700's,
drying live hides on racks of great ribs,

grinding grass into cud,
cud into rich blood rising from skulls
to darken thick bases of young horns,

pushing horn tips in slow motion
and twisting them through big Texas sky
like gnarled, timeless branches of mesquite.

They stand in Texas sun.
They push their horn tips.
They flaunt their sunstruck hides.

Up to His Armpit

in wet, steaming darkness,
using every lesson
he learned from farmers past,
he worked the thick tendons

of his fingers
struggling to right
twin calves for birthing.
His good cow died

sparing her twins,
and for days on end
he couldn't rid his arm
of the strong womb-stench,

stenciling his obtuse
manliness with the life-
and-death peril
of common motherhood.

Road Kill

It's as if they lay there
in the pattern of some dark plan,
spaced as they were on the macadam,
flattened by the sole of a jealous god
for imminent mummification by the sun,
a male and female jackrabbit
catching the corner of my eye at daybreak.

I couldn't help but picture the instant
before their deaths, their eyes all pupil
leading them through the ink black night,
making sudden contact with beams
so bright they had to be celestial,
leaving them hopelessly paralyzed
in the snapshot-quick of rapture.

III. OUT OF THE BLUE

It Was So Dry in Midland

far West Texas

even grown trees died
if they weren't watered.
Sunday afternoons, after church,

the embers of hell still crackling
like mesquite in our rapid
little jackrabbit hearts,

we'd pack into the Buick,
picnic sacks in tow,
and head with Mom to Cole Park.

There, three or four miles
outside the city limits,
they dug several deep wells

just to water the elms.
We could see their green for miles
rising from the flat horizon,

lining our waterless oasis,
incongruous with the desertscape
as whores standing in the baptistery.

West Texas Interlude

Just minutes before the blue
norther hit, the macadam
of Highway 80 gleamed
in the bright April sun,
stretched straight through the desert
as taut, black satin ribbon.
Dad had heard the warning

on the radio, stuffed us
into the back seat of his
'56 rose and black Ford,
and stormed out of Midland.
Out of nowhere, through clouds
grown suddenly green
and tufted, the cyclone

hit the desert floor
and tore right toward us
like the spun black top of God.
Though it danced over us,
that time, I'll never forget
the rear view mirror, blinding
with the whites of Dad's eyes.

Dewberries

They grew in brambles
along a barbed-wire fence.
Within days that summer
and right before our eyes,
like our own strange bodies
ripening with pubescence,
they'd turn from greenish-white

to pink, pink to red,
and red to dark purple.
The night after we picked them,
our tongues still blue with guilt,
the maps of our skin
covered with hundreds
of thin red highways

scribbled by their thorns,
and stinging, we'd picture,
before we fell asleep,
the buckets brimming with them
on Grandma's kitchen table,
pregnant with the promises
of muffins and a cobbler.

A Place in the Sun

When a dutiful child,
I sat on my pew with folded hands
like a strange piñata
layered with the onion-
skin pages of my Bible.

As I grew up, the layers
dried and cracked wide-open,
oozing the pungent
smelling salts of recognition,
drawing me up, against my will, smack dab

in the middle of communion,
from the hard oaken pew
of my chrysalis
and leading me down the aisle
to take my rightful place

in the sun, shocking the congregation
with my ostensible irreverence
though I stood in the bright hot light
more consonant with Jesus
than I'd ever been.

Of Fathers and Sons

One summer morning, an hour before first light,
when Mom and Dad thought I was asleep,
I awoke to the bubbling and the scent

of percolating Folgers and a portion
of soft conversation seeping ghostlike
through the thin wooden panel of my door.

The day before, Dad and I had argued
violently about his never telling me
he loved me. He said it was ludicrous,

that I should find more than adequate
his seven-day workweek at his filling station.
I blurted I didn't. He retorted, "Tough."

We then went back to work, he under
the grease rack, I in the carwash stall. I felt
hurt, started washing the cars harder.

In my bed, I heard him tell Mom how proud
of me he was, how he'd never seen a man
wash as many cars in a twelve-hour

day. It gave me chills, so much I just lay there
frozen till sunrise. Years later, moments before
their joint burial, I let them know I heard.

The Feather Duster

by itself saved Mama
from the terrible sin
of idleness.
In Midland, Texas,
our small backyard
was but a parcel
of Chihuahuan Desert,

much better suited
for horned lizards
than human beings.
I never understood
Brother Bell always
shouting that we "shall"
have returned to dust

when all the while he yelled
it abraded his eyes
and made a grating sound
between his gnashing teeth.
The wind, with nothing
standing in its way,
turned our Easter sky

into a swirling sandbox.
By the time Mama dusted
the third room
of our three-room house,
she couldn't even tell
she'd already dusted
the first.

Edward Wells

for Roy

The familiarity of his voice
belied "Edward Wells," the strange name
glowing on the screen of my caller ID.

He said the unlisted number
under his real name had become
public as a whore, turning up

distant relatives who kept calling,
idling the dull engines of their lives
on the fuel of nostalgia,

oblivious to the time
which had so marvelously
warped them into total strangers.

Said he wished them well,
enjoyed them forty or so years ago
when he sort of knew them,

and just wished they'd respect
the flowers they now were,
flattened in the middle of a book.

Said he hadn't the vaguest idea
how he'd come up with "Edward."
Said he must have figured

if it were good enough
for cigars and kings,
it'd surely do the trick for him.

The Night We Were Gods

They hung by thread
just above our heads
in the entryway,
five hummingbirds
of clear red glass

covered with glitter.
Absentmindedly,
we brushed them
with the tips
of our forefingers,

rubbed our eyelids
and smeared them
with galaxies
of tiny stars.
For several hours,

till we showered,
and never even
noticing, we blessed
everything we touched
with crushed light.

After Surgery

for Deena

From the deep, impassive
sleep of anesthesia,
she wakes to glare

and unimaginable
whiteness. The harsh word
of a nurse rules out heaven;

the cold, hell. Soon the ache,
subtle as a maniac
bringing down a dagger,

strikes, nailing her
to the rough-hewn cross
of a second chance.

She rises from her bed,
cross and all, drags
her wounds into the sun,

and just stands there, racked
with the gorgeous agony
of survival.

In the Studio

where poems emerge
from the skin of blank paper
like scabbed tattoos,

the bust of a cowhand
sits on an oaken
wagon wheel end table.

For years the cowhand's stared
at a sage sofa's arm,
intently as if

it belonged to a goddess.
A few feet to his left,
a Crow warrior

dances on a bookcase,
so fixed in his trance
he's turned to bronze.

High above and between them,
before a windowpane,
hangs a fruit-laden

stained-glass prickly pear,
so pregnant with sunlight
it creaks.

Blue Norther

At high noon,
brutal as a boot
kicked into the groin
of indolence,

it hits,
tattooing the cheeks
of cowhands
with frostbite,

locking the eyes
of hawks
wide-open
with a glaze

of clear blue ice
freezing their bodies
upright to the tops
of fence posts,

terrorizing
the bleak
West Texas
desertscape

like a huge
blue falcon
loosed from the wrist
of God.

The Hawk

I knew by its size
and the way
the doves scattered
it wasn't a crow
or boat-tailed grackle.

It landed in the top
of a pecan tree,
and perched there
for several minutes,
gazing at the heart

of the hamlet.
Its splayed tail
snatched the bullets
of the sun,
and smashed them

like the caps
of a toy pistol,
for its red.
The local jays
tried to bluff it

with the fierceness
of their squawking,
their bravery belied
but by the terrible
distances they kept.

Bluebonnets

for Suzie and Jim

Each April
they blanket
the landscape
like foot-
deep snow
where lovers flock
by the dozens,

spreading
their blankets
and reclining,
their bodies
gently bouncing
on the soft,
petaled springs,

buoyant
on the waves
of a stormless,
endless sea
where blue
is all
that matters.

The Nights

near Fort Davis
are so
unpolluted
with artificial
light
the stars
piled high

on the line
'twixt earth, sky,
shift
and sparkle;
so quiet
one who listens
hard enough

can hear
the swish
of rattlers
coiling
their necklaces
of dark
diamonds.

Out of the Blue

But for the three of us,
the park that day was deserted.
Mom meant no harm
and said she was just kidding
when, out of the blue,
she sped off in the Buick
and left me and my little brother
stranded on the blanket
we'd spread for a picnic.
Beyond the elm-shaded acres
of Cole Park, in far West Texas,
the flat red earth
ran unobstructed for miles
in all four directions
all the way to the horizon.
Sam clutched his teddy bear
and started crying.
I stood in my white,
suspendered shorts
and watched the car
dissolve in a cloud of dust.
A few minutes later,
when she drove back,
I was still standing,
too shocked to speak or cry,
dispossessed at three of my trust,
held against her heaving chest
weightless as the husk
of a cicada.

Bluing

It came in a little
bottle, so blue it looked
jet-black. I knew it was
nothing but trouble,
the way a tiny

drop of it would turn
a washtub of water
into a huge, sloshing
sapphire. Mama used it,
oddly enough, to whiten

our Sunday shirts.
Over time it bled
right through her skin
and blued her all the way
to commitment

in the Wichita State
Hospital, bleaching
her heart into a locket
white and fragile
as fine bone china.

To Blue

in memory of Samuel E. Thomas

in bleak December,
he loosed his restless soul.
For days before he died,
his frail body
propped on a cane,

he scoured countless stores
and antique shops
for blue glass ornaments.
He hung them
on a noble fir

flocked snow-white,
strung with endless
strands of blue lights,
and slept on a cot
beside the tree.

As death descended
in a flock of blue crows,
his blue eyes glistened
with legions of blue angels
blaring their silent horns.

The Sky

over Taos
is over-
powering, so blue
it's palpable,

a mammoth
rolling pin
flattening in time
the dough of adobes,

the crust of the stark
white cross.
Flush with the earth
it looms,

gloving the living
with its blue,
allowing them nothing,
not even a wispy

cloud of gauze,
between themselves
and their fathomless
cobalt destinies.

IV. WITH THE HAND OF THE GREAT SPIRIT

Mesquite

Tornadoes
but gnarl
your brutal trunk

and drive
your mile-deep roots
even deeper,

tightening
your grip on hell,
your wood so hard

it ruins the teeth
of chain saws,
never fooled

by a late freeze,
the last
of living things

to green out
in the spring,
growing great beans

the Comanches chewed
to soothe
their ravaged bowels.

Kaleidoscope

morning in Santa Fe
of breathtaking brightness
when even the petals

of the flowers children pluck
are stained glass ablaze with sunlight
and the sky pulsates in the bathed,

inscrutable eyes of young women;
when adulterers luxuriate
under the chocolate gaze of a priest

and the bronze, wrinkled skin
of Indians blooms silver
studded with chunks of polished turquoise;

when, rising in their homes of adobe,
the old women open their shutters
and gasp in flashfloods of light.

Pottery Seller

for Doug and Linda

Warm with Arizona sun,
its sacred interior
awash with shadow
so black it breathes,
a piece of pottery

is cradled in the hand
of an old Navajo woman.
Her fingers are ringed
with untarnished silver
in which are swaddled

shards of purest sky.
She manages a toothless smile,
easing her art skyward
into the spidery grip
of a buyer.

In a muffled
rush of wind,
it exits her flesh
and a whole nation
gasps in quiet recoil.

Kachinas

To prepare them for a brush
of stiff yucca fiber,
for the red, yellow, white,
gray, blue-green and black

painstakingly extracted
from vegetable, iron oxide
and an ore of copper,
a color for each of the six

cardinal directions, the Hopi
carved them from cottonwood root
with a flake of stone and sanded them
for a coat of finest clay.

With the hand of the Great Spirit,
they adorned them with the down
of eagles, wisps of owl fluff,
and the feathers of birds of prey.

Canyon de Chelly

for Lisa

In a certain place where the canyon wall
meets the sand of the canyon floor

at a forty-five degree angle, an aged
Navajo woman is weaving a basket

under a canyon wall streaked with stains
of ancient rain, a massive canyon wall

rising hundreds of feet above the deft
maneuvering of her fingers in a quiet place

where the scream of a long dead hawk
echoes in a timeless ricochet

in this certain place where the Navajo
live whole lives buried beautifully alive

in a sacred grave packed with the breathing
sand of sky and turquoise desert air.

In Dinehtah

the sacred homeland of the Navajo

the women
are sleeping
in wombs of logs, brush,
and sun-dried earth.

The women
are dreaming
of their sheep
grazing in the cold

mountain night,
steeping thick wool
in starlight, moonglow,
for the intricate looms

of deepest lineage.
Ever-so-close
to their lips,
their bronze hands,

darkened with hues
of natural dyes,
are splayed
on wool blankets

where braids
of thick hair
are coiled
like black rattlers.

As the women sleep,
their deep
and even breathing,
sweetened

with fresh corn,
mists the sky-
blue stones
of their ancient rings.

Grandmother Thomas

in memory of Isabelle Wright Thomas

She came to live with us
shortly before she died.
Her skin tone was brown
as the cotton stockings
whose tops she rolled down
just below her knees.
She had high cheekbones,

angular as the rest
of her tall, gaunt frame.
At least half-Indian,
she cringed when asked
about her bloodline,
whether she were Cherokee
or some other tribe.

She'd been taught that they
were savages, half-human,
that she should deny
an ounce of their blood.
Nights, when her light went out,
I'd creep to her room,
lie down, and listen

with my ear to the space
beneath her door.
I'd hear her muffled
chanting, oozing like the coos
of doves, the Great Spirit
washing over me
like mild fever.

V. FROM THE ROLL UP YONDER

Mule Trader

in memory of Charles Franklin Thomas

Before his retirement,
his knobby fingers reeked
of the drool of mules
whose mouths he pried open
to glance at their teeth,
extracting their age
to perfection. In his
golden years, too old
to fiddle with the mouths

of mules, he whittled cowboys
with his pocket knife
from thin, flat pieces
of pine. He'd suspend them
on twisted cotton string
between two sticks
joined by a brace
at their centers. When one
squeezed the sticks, the cowboys

flipped back and forth
like acrobats,
as if he knew
the time would soon come
when the valiant
cowboy of his youth
would pass to legend,
put out to the pasture
of tricks and movies.

The Cisco Kid

in memory of Margaret Ann Elizabeth Cisco Coleman

It came on the same time
each week, Mama Sug's
favorite Western TV show.
She'd get so excited
watching it, Mother
was concerned for her heart.

I'll never forget the way
she riveted her pale blue eyes
to the black-and-white screen,
squinting to see the characters,
the bad cowboys in black hats,
the good ones in white.

Though the good guys always won,
one would never have known it
by watching Mama Sug,
tense as a convict
in the electric chair,
waiting for the flip of the switch.

After she fell and broke her hip,
it was the only thread
that pulled her from one
brutal week to the next.
I didn't know till she died
her maiden name was Cisco.

Jake

in memory of Rufus Andrew Coleman

He and Mama Sug
passed their idle time
fishing tanks with cane poles
for crappie and perch.
His back bowed from years
of plowing fields with mules
and fathering ten children,
he never complained
and hardly ever spoke.

Though he had but one good lung,
I never saw him sans
a hand-rolled cigarette
dangling from his lips,
lumpy as Mama Sug's
homemade soap. For forty years,
after she got religion,
Mama hounded him
to get baptized. Finally,

just before he died
at eighty-five, to shut
Mama up, he gave in
and was dunked. As soon
as he got home, he rolled
himself a Prince Albert
and snuck a swig of Old Crow
he'd kept hidden for years
for such a sweet occasion.

Aunt Mae and Uncle Worley's Rocker

For the last ten years of his life,
in rain or shine, he shuffled
to his rocker on the porch
to while away his hours.

It sits in the same place
it sat when he died a decade back.
Its presence comforts her:
the way the slats of its seat

slightly sag as if still laden
with his weight; the way at night,
when the wind's just right,
a floorboard creaks with its rocking.

She's left it there to play out
its usefulness, to play with the sun,
in the tournament of dust,
the checkers of light and shadow.

Checkers

Stooped and hobbled with arthritis,
they rise everyday
an hour before first light,
don khaki trousers suspendered

to their rickety collarbones,
breakfast with wives they seldom
look at or let alone speak to,
and shuffle to shadowy halls

near the squares of their hamlets.
On wooden whiskey barrels
scooted to the edges
of makeshift tables,

they while away their hours
playing fellow townsmen
who've screwed them
and whom they've screwed,

in business and in bed,
exacting, with their magical
little disks of red and black,
their sweet revenge.

Alzheimer's

She first heard its onset
in the sudden, staccato
rhythm of her speech,
in the gradual diminishing
of brilliant memory

from chord to arpeggio.
Though largely confined
to the minimalist composition
of her nursing home room,
she still insists that the aide

help her daily with a black gown
and wrap her hair in a bun.
Positioned on her bench
with the straight-backed posture
she assumed as a concert pianist,

she sits at her only window
and watches the diminuendo of light
from afternoon to evening,
evening to dusk and dusk
to the endlessly repeated

étude of the night,
each of her long,
slender fingers
swaying like the winding down
needle of a metronome.

Texas Two-Step

For sixty some odd years,
he worked cattle. His backbone's
bowed like a divining rod
urgent for water,
pulling his face toward the dust.

Having outlived all his children,
he still somehow manages
to live alone. In far West Texas,
in the land of his ancestors,
he lives in his centenarian

world where dreams and consciousness
are partners in a polka.
Nights, prior to retiring,
after the wind has died
and dust has settled

on his corrugated iron roof
like the laying on of hands,
he shoves his boots
under the cane-bottomed chair
beside his bed.

Mornings, regaining consciousness
like a slowly developing
negative, he neither knows nor cares,
till his boots come into focus,
whether he's still in the dance.

Church Organist

Against a backdrop of sunset, the chollas
jut into the sky like clusters of old

rugged crosses. As she's done each rainless
evening since her retirement, she takes her place

in her porch rocker, pulls down her lower lip,
packs with a flat wooden spoon a dip

of snuff, and starts rocking. Notes of "Amazing
Grace," the last hymn she played before conceding

to the narrowing angles of arthritis,
swirl in her memories like dust

in a shaft of sunlight. She bends
her good ear to the wind,

straining to hear, drawing ever closer,
the names from the roll up yonder.